INTRO TO
HORSE RACING

BY WHITNEY SANDERSON

SADDLE UP!

SportsZone

An Imprint of Abdo Publishing
abdopublishing.com

abdopublishing.com

Published by Abdo Publishing, a division of ABDO, PO Box 398166, Minneapolis, Minnesota 55439. Copyright © 2018 by Abdo Consulting Group, Inc. International copyrights reserved in all countries. No part of this book may be reproduced in any form without written permission from the publisher. SportsZone™ is a trademark and logo of Abdo Publishing.

Printed in the United States of America, North Mankato, Minnesota
092017
012018

Cover Photo: Shutterstock Images
Interior Photos: Shutterstock Images, 1; Michael Adamucci/USA Today Sports/Newscom, 5; Jon Durr/ESW/Cal Sport Media/AP Images, 6–7; Cliff Welch/Icon Sportswire, 8–9; Joshua Sarner/Icon Sportswire, 11; Bill Kostroun/AP Images, 12–13; Hulton Archive/Getty Images, 15; Lillis Photography/iStockphoto, 16–17; Kelly Van Dellen/iStockphoto, 18–19; Blaine Harrington/Age Fotostock/SuperStock, 20–21; Mint Images/SuperStock, 24; Patrick Semansky/AP Images, 27; Chad Palmer/Shutterstock Images, 29; John Minchillo/AP Images, 31; Hagen Hopkins/Getty Images Sport/Getty Images, 32–33; Stefan Holm/Shutterstock Images, 34–35; Cheryl Ann Quigley/Shutterstock Images, 37; Rob Carr/Getty Images Sport/Getty Images, 39; Charles Bertram/ZumaPress/Newscom, 40; Garry Jones/AP Images, 43; Rex Features/AP Images, 44

Editor: Marie Pearson
Series Designer: Laura Polzin
Content Consultant: Paige Clark, B.S. Equine Science, University of Minnesota Crookston

Publisher's Cataloging-in-Publication Data
Names: Sanderson, Whitney, author.
Title: Intro to horse racing / by Whitney Sanderson.
Description: Minneapolis, Minnesota : Abdo Publishing, 2018. | Series: Saddle up! | Includes online resources and index.
Identifiers: LCCN 2017946884 | ISBN 9781532113420 (lib.bdg.) | ISBN 9781532152306 (ebook)
Subjects: LCSH: Horse Racing--Juvenile literature. | Horsemanship--Juvenile literature. | Horse sports--Juvenile literature.
Classification: DDC 798.4--dc23
LC record available at https://lccn.loc.gov/2017946884

TABLE OF
CONTENTS

1

A NEW CROWN

On June 6, 2015, the racetrack at Belmont Park in New York was packed with 90,000 people. They came to watch a horse named American Pharoah race in the Belmont Stakes. The horse with the misspelled name had already won the Kentucky Derby on the first Saturday in May and the Preakness Stakes two weeks later.

Together, these three races are known as the Triple Crown. They are open only to 3-year-old Thoroughbreds. Winning all three races is one of the most sought-after goals in the sport of horse racing. Only 11 horses had done

it, beginning with Sir Barton in 1919. The most recent winner, Affirmed, beat his rival Alydar in each race to capture the crown in 1978.

American Pharoah certainly looked like a winner. The big, muscular bay strutted through the paddock with his long, swinging stride and a confident gaze. He had already achieved more than his sire, or father, Pioneer of the Nile, who placed second in the Kentucky Derby in 2009.

American Pharoah had an impressive team of humans working with him, too. His owner, Ahmed Zayat, was an Egyptian-American entrepreneur who ran the multimillion dollar Zayat Stables.

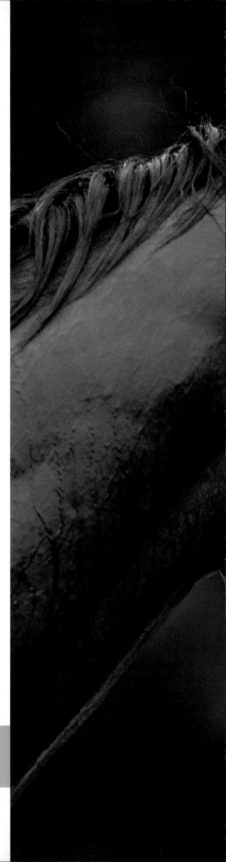

Ahmed Zayat gives American Pharoah a kiss the day before the Belmont Stakes.

The horses in the Belmont Stakes took off from the gate. American Pharoah was number five.

His trainer was Bob Baffert, who in 2015 won his fourth Eclipse Award as the top trainer in the country. His jockey was Victor Espinoza. He won the first two races of the Triple Crown a year earlier on a chestnut colt named California Chrome.

But American Pharoah's victory in the Belmont was far from certain. The last jewel in the Triple Crown is the hardest to capture. Many horses that can keep up their speed over the 1.25-mile Derby and the 1.2-mile Preakness don't have the stamina to win over the Belmont's longer distance of 1.5 miles. And some racing experts say that horses bred today are too closely matched in ability for any horse to win all three races.

Could American Pharoah prove them wrong? He was a 5-to-7 favorite to win. That means someone betting on American Pharoah would have to bet $7 in order to get $5 if he won.

Track announcer Larry Collmus called the race. He described the action over a loudspeaker so that people in the grandstand or those watching on TV could tell how the race was unfolding.

Eight horses and jockeys approached the starting gate. One by one, each pair was led into a narrow, padded stall. Every horse had an assigned post position. American Pharoah was number 5. There was a short pause once all the horses had settled in. Then the starting gates sprung open and Collmus said, "They're off in the Belmont Stakes!"

American Pharoah was slow to break from the gate. Espinoza still managed to send him on to an early lead with another colt, Materiality, close on his heels. Keen Ice, Mubtaahij, and Frosted were not far behind.

By the halfway mark, American Pharoah was still three-quarters of a length ahead of Materiality. Then American Pharoah seemed to find another gear. He began to pull away from the field.

American Pharoah hung on to his early lead.

Heading toward the finish line, a colt named Frosted edged into second place. For a moment, it looked like he might challenge the leader. But he couldn't gain any ground on American Pharoah.

Collmus's voice rose to a shout as the bay colt thundered down the final furlong, five and a half lengths ahead of Frosted. The rest of the field was even farther behind. The crowd was already erupting into cheers.

"And here it is, the 37-year wait is over!" cried Collmus. "American Pharoah is finally the one. . . . American Pharoah has won the Triple Crown!"

Espinoza celebrated the win when he and American Pharoah raced past the finish line.

RACING THROUGH HISTORY

The boast "my horse is faster than your horse!" has probably been heard since people first tamed wild horses more than 6,000 years ago. In ancient Rome, chariot races were a popular form of entertainment. In later centuries, any horse owner could challenge another to a race down Main Street. People from town would gather to watch, with some betting any spare change in their pockets.

FOUNDING FATHERS

All Thoroughbreds are descended from three foundation sires: the Darley Arabian, the Byerley Turk, and the Godolphin Arabian. In 1791 James Weatherby of England created the General Stud Book to keep track of which stallions were bred to which mares. In 1873 an American stud book began. Today the Jockey Club oversees Thoroughbred breeding and racing.

Horse racing began as an organized sport in England in the 1700s. Large sums of money were needed to breed and train the best horses, so racing became known as "the sport of kings."

In the last century, horse racing has become a highly technical sport. Owners, trainers, and veterinarians use the latest science and technology to get the most out of their horses. But the goal of racing has never changed. Everyone on the track is trying to find that special, fast horse to outrun the competition and perhaps capture the Triple Crown. Not every trainer is lucky enough to come across a horse of American Pharoah's talent. But winning the Triple Crown is the ultimate racing dream.

An artist depicted a race between the Duke of Somerset's horse and the Duke of Bolton's horse in the early 1700s.

SCHOOL DAYS: THE FIRST TWO YEARS

Many American racehorses are bred in or near Lexington, Kentucky. Although it's probably a folktale, some trainers believe that the famous Kentucky bluegrass helps young horses build stronger bones than those raised elsewhere. Thoroughbred breeding is carefully planned. The owner hopes to produce a foal that has the best qualities of its sire and dam, or mother. A mare that is a fast sprinter and a stallion that has the ability to run long distances might be paired.

age

The hope would be that their foal will have both speed and stamina.

Mares carry their foals for approximately 11 months. A healthy foal is able to stand within minutes and gallop within hours of its birth. Foals are born with legs nearly as long as they will be when the horse is fully grown. Male foals are called colts, and female foals are called fillies. Beginning at age 4, they are known as stallions and mares.

The official birthday of all Thoroughbred horses is January 1. Thoroughbreds race against other horses born in the same calendar year. Mares are bred so they will foal as early in the year as possible. A 3-year-old born in January will

Thoroughbred foals can run with their mothers soon after they are born.

have an advantage in strength and experience when racing a 3-year-old born in November or December.

Grooms are responsible for the daily care of Thoroughbreds on a farm. They keep close watch over pregnant mares. They may help with births. They get young horses used to being led, brushed, bathed, and held for the vet. On most farms, mares and foals are turned out in groups to graze and socialize. They are grouped by age and sex. Thoroughbreds are often competitive from the beginning, racing each other across the pasture.

Young Thoroughbreds must be registered with the Jockey Club before they can race. Each horse

Grooms teach foals to be led by walking them with their mothers.

gets a tattoo on the inside of its upper lip to help prevent theft and to identify the horses.

GROWING UP

Thoroughbred foals are weaned, or separated from their dams, when they are approximately six months old. Many colts and fillies are sold as yearlings, a term for 1-year-olds. The most famous yearling sale is the Keeneland September auction in Lexington, Kentucky. Some horses are bought by individual owners. Others are purchased by groups of people who share the horse's cost and earnings.

At around 18 months of age, Thoroughbreds are ready to start training. Some breeding farms have tracks, but many young horses are sent to special training stables.

TRAINING

The first few times the horse is ridden, the rider often sits quietly while a handler leads the horse. After the horse gets used to carrying the weight, it will learn how to respond to cues from the rider's reins, seat, legs, and voice. Some Thoroughbreds take to being ridden more easily than others. The legendary racehorse Man O' War was known for being difficult to train, often rearing up and throwing his rider.

The first few times it is ridden, a young horse will only be walked and jogged. Later the rider will take the horse for slow gallops around a training track. These workouts are planned by a trainer, who decides how quickly to move the horse along based on its fitness and ability. People who ride Thoroughbreds in their daily workouts are called exercise riders. Jockeys are the riders for races. Exercise riders can be anyone who can ride, but jockeys must be small and skilled at riding in race conditions.

WHAT'S IN A NAME?

A Thoroughbred's registered name must have fewer than 18 letters. It can't be the name of a famous racehorse or the name of a winner of an important race in the past 25 years. The Jockey Club also doesn't allow names that serve as advertising. You won't find any racehorses called Built Ford Tough or Enjoy A Pepsi.

When the trainer decides the horse is ready, the rider will move up to fast workouts called breezes. Running handily is even faster, close to racing speed. This begins

to really test the horse's potential. At first the horse will only be asked to work handily for a few furlongs at a time. Most 2-year-olds work up to a full mile, the distance of many races. The trainer will also have the horse practice running in groups to encourage its instinct to win. Many Thoroughbreds seem to love to run, and these are often the most successful racehorses.

The final task is teaching the horse to break from the starting gate. Many horses are nervous about the gate at first and need quite a few sessions before they are comfortable standing in the enclosed stall. Then they must practice galloping off with increasing speed when the gates open. By the time a 2-year-old has finished these lessons, it is ready to race.

Exercise tracks are not as fancy as racetracks.

BEHIND THE SCENES ON THE RACETRACK

Horses usually arrive at the track a few days before they are scheduled to race. This gives them time to recover from traveling and get used to the environment. Horses exercise on the track in the mornings. A track official times them and combines workout times with a horse's past performances to help set betting odds.

The area of the track that includes the stables is called the backside. It is closed to the public. The seating area for the audience is called the grandstand. People might pay extra for a pass to the clubhouse area, where they

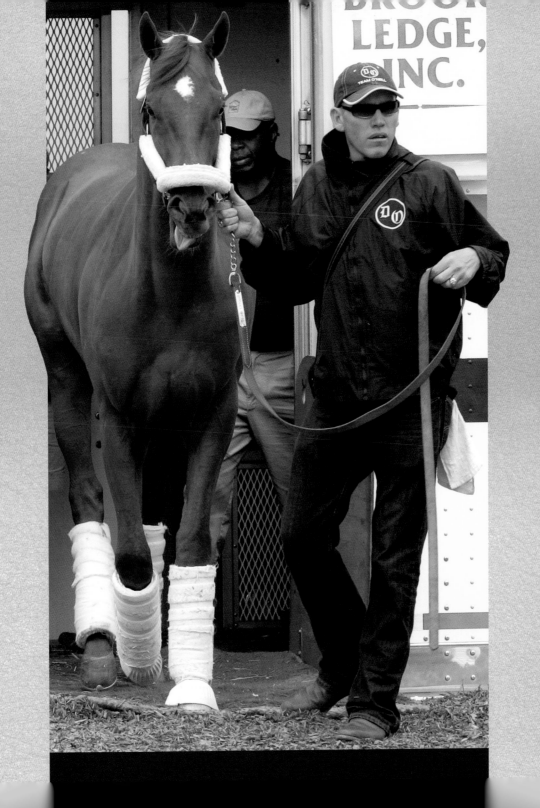

can sit in private boxes and host parties. The horses are saddled outside in an area called the paddock. People can gather around the rail and see the horses up close before they race.

Racetracks can vary in size, but they are always oval in shape with a rail on both sides. The homestretch is the straight side of the track in front of the grandstand. The more distant straightaway is called the backstretch. The finish line is always near the end of the homestretch so the audience has a clear view.

TYPES OF RACES

Races are often open to horses of a certain age and sex, such as a race for 2-year-old colts or for mares 5 and up. Most races are held on dirt tracks, but some are on turf courses, which have a grass surface.

At the Churchill Downs racetrack, people can watch from the grandstand, *right,* or from the middle of the track, called the infield.

Maiden races are for horses that have never won. Once a horse "breaks its maiden" by placing first, it will move up to running in races with more prize money. The prize is called a purse. Graded stakes are the highest-paying races. They also have the toughest competition.

Handicapping allows horses of different abilities to run together by having the fastest horses carry more weight.

A track handicapper looks at each horse's past performances to decide how much to assign. Not all races have handicaps. In the Kentucky Derby, every colt carries 126 pounds (57.2 kg) and every filly carries 121 pounds (55.9 kg). This weight includes the jockey.

Three-year-old fillies have their own version of the Kentucky Derby. They race each other in the Kentucky Oaks at the Churchill Downs racetrack. But some fillies run with the boys. Three fillies have won the Kentucky Derby: Regret in 1915, Genuine Risk in 1980, and Winning Colors in 1988.

GIRL POWER

Colts and stallions tend to be bigger and faster on average than fillies, but there have been many excellent female racehorses. One of the best is Zenyatta, a dark bay mare that won 19 out of 20 races from 2007 to 2010.

PLAYING THE ODDS

Betting has long been paired with horse racing. There are many different types of bets. The simplest is a win bet.

Filly Abel Tasman won the 2017 Kentucky Oaks.

The bettor gets money if his or her chosen horse wins the race. A show bet means that horse must finish first, second, or third. The minimum bet is usually $2. The money from bets is pooled and then paid out after the race. The payments are based on the official odds. If a horse was not likely to win but did, those who bet on it to win would get more money than if the horse had been expected to win. The horse most likely to win is called the favorite. A horse considered unlikely to win is called a long shot.

GETTING READY

Before each race, the jockeys are weighed while carrying their horses' tack, which is gear such as the

Jockeys and tack must be weighed both before and after the race to make sure no one cheated by removing weight.

33

bridle and saddle. If the number is lower than the weight officials say the horse needs to carry, the horse must wear a heavier saddle pad. Racing saddles are very light so the horse can move freely. A square saddlecloth with a number in the corner shows the horse's gate position for the race.

Some horses wear extra gear to keep them focused. Blinkers keep the horse from seeing anything that is not straight ahead. Shadow rolls keep the horse from looking down and getting distracted by its shadow. If a horse is sensitive to loud sounds such as cheering from a grandstand,

Blinkers, *center*, and shadow rolls, *left*, keep horses focused on racing.

it might wear earplugs. American Pharoah wore them for the Kentucky Derby.

The jockey wears a bright, lightweight outfit called silks. Its colors show which stable he or she is riding for. Each pattern is unique to a certain owner. The jockey may also carry a short whip. Rules limit how many times the whip can be used during a race.

Once the horses are saddled, the paddock judge calls, "Riders up!" and the jockeys mount their horses. The horses walk from the paddock to the track, where they jog and canter to warm up. Riders on calm horses called lead ponies stay next to the racehorses to keep them calm.

In the post parade, the horses jog past the grandstand in single file so the crowd can have a final look at them. Outriders on horses stand by, ready to help with feisty horses or catch any that may get loose. As the horses approach the starting gate, the lead ponies are left behind. Track employees help load each horse into a stall. The starter pushes a button so all the gates spring open together.

GEAR

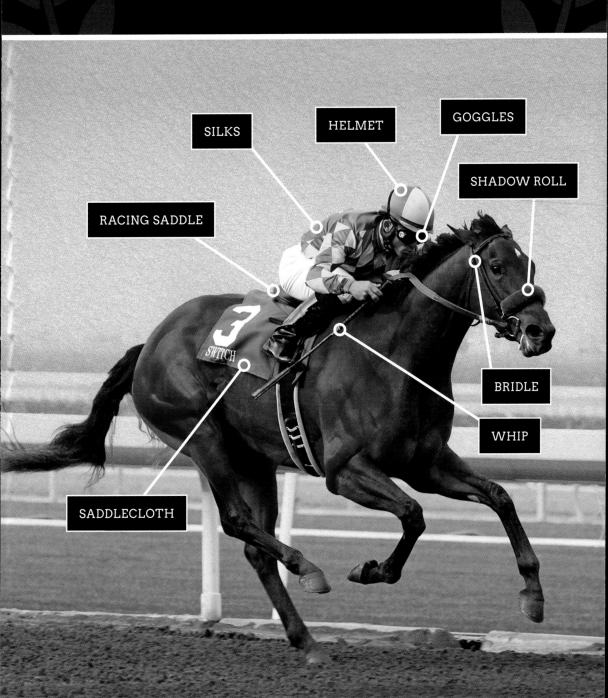

4

THE LIFE OF A RACEHORSE

Before each race, the trainer always discusses a running strategy with the jockey. But some things can change the plan. The footing on the track might be different than expected, or the horse might be bumped or crowded. The jockey must be able to make decisions quickly. Things can change fast with horses running at 40 miles per hour (64 km/h).

Each horse tends to have a natural running style. Some like to take the lead early. Others would rather stay in the middle of the pack until they make their move. A few

Jockey Kevin Krigger, *left,* and trainer Doug O'Neil discuss race plans after a morning workout.

prefer to close from behind in the last few furlongs.

Motion-sensing cameras at the finish line take an official picture of the winner. A very close race is called a photo finish because the track announcer may be unable to tell who won. The picture gives the final answer.

RACING RISKS

Horse racing is an exciting sport but also a dangerous one. Serious injury and death are a possibility for both horses and jockeys. Accidents are usually caused by interference (when one horse bumps another) or by injury. Horses have fragile legs that sometimes break down under the stress of racing.

A MOMENT OF GLORY

After the race, the winning horse and jockey head to the winner's circle. People take photos with the owner and trainer. Following a big race such as the Kentucky Derby, journalists might interview everyone involved with the horse's training.

The purse can range from a few thousand dollars to several million. For the Kentucky Derby, the top five

Always Dreaming, ridden by John R. Velazquez, won the 2017 Kentucky Derby.

finishers divide a purse of $2 million. After the race, the winning horse is tested to make sure that it was not given illegal drugs or other substances to improve its run.

Back at the stable, a groom or a machine—both called a hot walker—walks the horse. The machine has moving arms which horses are tied to. It walks horses in circles until they cool down. A groom gives the horse sips of water every few minutes, followed by a cool bath. Sometimes special tools such as ice boots are used to help the horse recover from the strain of the race. Ice boots are leg wraps filled with ice or frozen gel. They keep a horse's legs from swelling after a run. The horse returns to its stall for a clump of hay. It is hungry since it raced on an empty stomach. This is to keep it from having an upset stomach. After a race, the horse has a few weeks to rest and train before racing again. Most racehorses eat high-protein grain mixtures along with vitamins to keep them in top shape.

Baths help a horse cool off because the horse's body heat moves to the water, which is then wiped off.

AS THE YEARS GO BY

A racehorse's career is fairly short. Thoroughbreds retire from 5 to 10 years old. Many horses live well into their 20s. Racehorses often have injuries, especially to their legs or hooves, that take them off the track for good. Others are retired when they start slowing down or if they never raced well to begin with.

The best racehorses usually retire to careers as studs or broodmares. But geldings and horses with poor race records often face uncertain futures. Many ex-racehorses end up being sold cheaply at auction. Today the racing industry is making efforts to provide for Thoroughbreds after retirement. The Thoroughbred Aftercare Alliance is an organization that helps find new homes for horses off the track. Many Thoroughbreds go on to successful second careers in sports such as show jumping, eventing, and dressage. Even horses that were not great racers can excel at another sport.

Retired racers can become excellent mounts for many sports, including more unusual ones such as hunting with eagles.

GLOSSARY

BAY

A horse with a brown coat and a black mane and tail.

BET

To risk losing money for the chance to gain more based on the outcome of an event, such as a horse race.

BLINKERS

Leather or plastic cups attached to a hood or bridle to prevent a horse from seeing objects to the sides.

BRED

Caused to produce offspring.

FOOTING

The condition of the ground beneath the horse.

FURLONG

A distance equal to 0.125 miles (0.2 km).

GELDING

A male horse that has been surgically made unable to reproduce.

LENGTH

A measurement equal to the length of a horse.

MARE

A female horse.

RETIRE

To finish working in a career.

SHADOW ROLL

A thick piece of fleece placed over a horse's noseband to block its view of the ground directly ahead.

STALLION

A male horse that is able to reproduce.

STAMINA

A horse's ability to do work without tiring.

ONLINE RESOURCES

Booklinks
NONFICTION NETWORK
FREE! ONLINE NONFICTION RESOURCES

To learn more about horse racing, visit **abdobooklinks.com**. These links are routinely monitored and updated to provide the most current information available.

MORE INFORMATION

BOOKS

Buckley, James, Jr. *Who Was Seabiscuit?* New York: Grosset & Dunlap, 2015.

Harris, Susan E. *The United States Pony Club Manual of Horsemanship: Basics for Beginners/D Level.* Hoboken, NJ: Wiley, 2012.

Mickle, Shelley Fraser. *American Pharoah: Triple Crown Champion.* New York: Aladdin, 2017.

INDEX

ABOUT THE AUTHOR

Whitney Sanderson grew up riding horses as a member of a
4-H club and competing in local jumping and dressage shows.
She has written several books in the Horse Diaries chapter
book series. She is also the author of *Horse Rescue: Treasure*,
which is based on her time volunteering at an equine rescue
farm. She lives in Massachusetts.